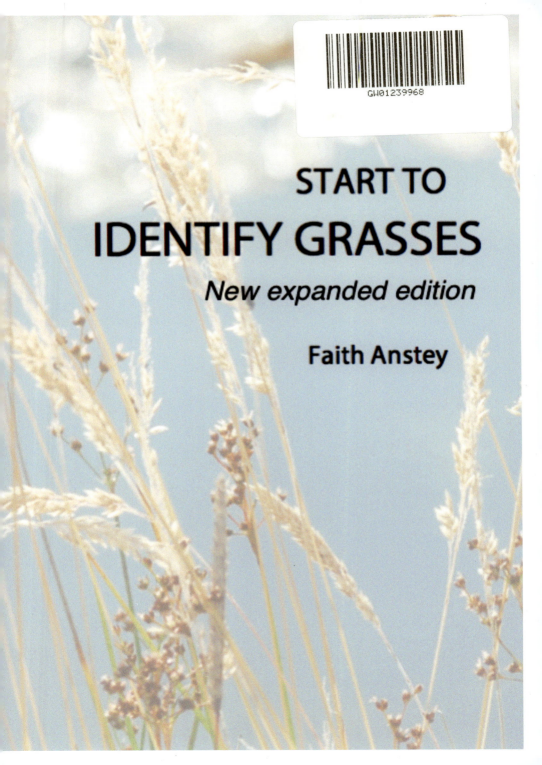

START TO
IDENTIFY GRASSES

New expanded edition

Faith Anstey

START TO
IDENTIFY GRASSES

Image by kind permission of Sarah Lambert © BSBI

Copyright © Faith Anstey 2018
New expanded edition 2020

Compiled in Word for Mac and set in Myriad Pro
Published by Wildflower Study
www.wildflowerstudy.co.uk
ISBN 978-0-9934933-4-8
Printed by Alliance Print Group

A note about images: although I have tried my best to avoid this, it is possible that some of the images used in this little book - gathered in various ways over several years – are, unbeknown to me, copyright or requiring credit. If you know this to be the case, please get in touch and I will make recompense and/or replace the image in the next edition.

START TO IDENTIFY GRASSES

Like its predecessor, the *Pocket Guide to Wildflower Families*, this booklet was originally composed for a BSBI (Scotland) workshop. In this case the workshop was on identifying common grasses, aimed at people with a basic knowledge of field botany, who nevertheless found grasses somewhat challenging. As no absolutely basic guide to grass ID existed, it then seemed a good idea to make the booklet available on general sale. This new expanded edition doubles the size of the original and includes some new material.

Running these workshops has made me acutely aware of what I have dubbed 'kleidophobia' – the fear of keys! Grass keys, such as those found in the classic work 'Hubbard' (see booklist on page 24) are particularly daunting, even for experts. So there are no keys in this book. Nor do you need a microscope to carry out the ID steps within it – a 10x lens should be quite adequate, as field characters are the only ones used.

To avoid the intimidating keys and microscopes, then, we concentrate here on just twenty species of grass, those which are by almost all measures the twenty most common grasses of neutral grassland in the British Isles.

CONTENTS

COMMON GRASSES OF NEUTRAL GRASSLAND

There seem to be three things that make identifying grasses difficult. In the first place, they don't have petals you can count, colours you can categorise or leaves that are easily distinguished – they are at first sight so 'samey'. Secondly, the keys used for identifying them have a whole new glossary of terms, and initially appear to be extraordinarily complicated. And finally, there are just so many of them to contend with – about 160 native British grass species.

So I am hoping here to help you walk before you try to run. This booklet introduces you to a mere 20 grass species: those you are most likely to find in **neutral grassland**. That is, the terrain is grassland as opposed to woodland, heath, bogs, saltmarshes or rocky mountains. It might be a meadow or rough grazing, roadside verge, forest clearing, cliff top, neglected garden, churchyard or something similar. And the habitat is neutral as opposed to particularly acid (peat bog, moorland etc) or particularly base-rich (chalkland, limestone pavement and so on).

These 20 are far and away the most commonly encountered in this kind of habitat. So much so, that if you find anything that is not dealt with here, then it is well worth studying further either the grass or the habitat, or both. One advantage of a sound knowledge of these 20 is that you will immediately be aware when something is *not* one of these. Then you may have to embark on keys, or the advice of an expert, to decide which grass it is.

BUT WHAT IS A GRASS?

Even though they have no showy petals, grasses are ==flowering plants==. (They don't need insect-attracting flowers because they are wind-pollinated.) Flowering plants fall into two main groups, colloquially known as **dicots** and **monocots**. ==Monocots== have a single seed-leaf, flower-parts in multiples of three (e.g. 3 petals, 3 sepals) and simple leaves which are usually blade-like, with parallel veins. Orchids, lilies and daffodils are monocots – and so are grasses, sedges and rushes. The last three can be grouped together as ==graminoids==. The rest – in other words, everything except the graminoids – are the ==forbs==.

The first diagram (page 6) 'Four Kinds of Monocot', shows you the basic distinctions between forbs (orchids, lilies etc) and the other three. Note, for example, that only grasses have ==nodes== up a stem which is both round and hollow. The grass leaf is in two parts – ==sheath and blade==. And grasses have a single inflorescence composed of spikelets.

The diagram on page 7 is a flowchart to separate grasses, sedges and rushes from each other. Note that one or two members of each group may not key out precisely from this flowchart – it is simply a handy guide while you find your feet, as it were.

So before you start your attempt to identify a grass, make sure that's what it is! Some rushes and sedges look superficially quite similar to grasses, but this book only deals with grasses. (There is a companion volume to this booklet called 'Start To Identify Sedges & Rushes'. You can get it from the website www.wildflowerstudy.co.uk.) Also remember the habitat caveat – if the grass you are wanting to ID was found in woodland, or in a bog or up a mountain, it is rather less likely to be found in this book (although a few related species from other habitats do get a brief mention).

FOUR KINDS OF MONOCOT

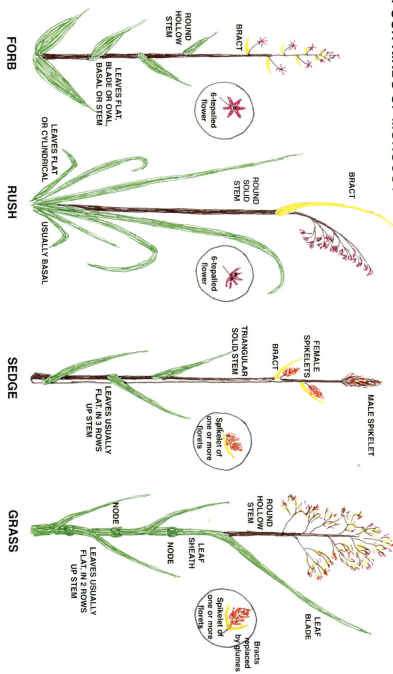

FORB

- ROUND HOLLOW STEM
- LEAVES FLAT, BLADE OR OVAL, BASAL OR STEM
- BRACT
- 6-tepalled flower

RUSH

- ROUND SOLID STEM
- LEAVES FLAT OR CYLINDRICAL USUALLY BASAL
- BRACT
- 6-tepalled flower

SEDGE

- TRIANGULAR SOLID STEM
- FEMALE SPIKELETS
- BRACT
- MALE SPIKELET
- LEAVES USUALLY FLAT, IN 3 ROWS UP STEM
- Spikelet of one or more florets

GRASS

- ROUND HOLLOW STEM
- NODE
- NODE
- LEAF SHEATH
- LEAVES USUALLY FLAT, IN 2 ROWS UP STEM
- LEAF BLADE
- Spikelet of one or more florets
- Bracts replaced by glumes

These are not diagrams of any particular species – they are typified examples.
The colours are diagrammatic – not necessarily true to life.
The different colours represent roughly equivalent parts in each kind of monocot, so that you can compare them.
Thus grasses have glumes instead of bracts, and the stem consists of interserted leaves.

6

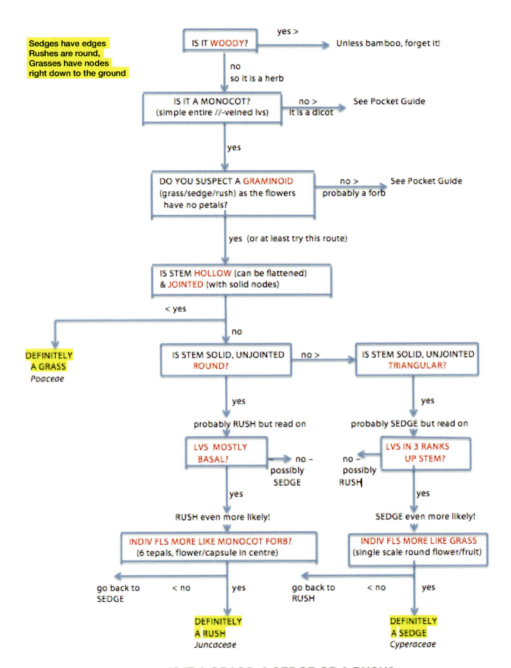

**Sedges have edges
Rushes are round,
Grasses have nodes
right down to the ground**

IS IT WOODY?
yes > Unless bamboo, forget it!

no
so it is a herb

IS IT A MONOCOT?
(simple entire //-veined lvs)
no > See Pocket Guide
it is a dicot

yes

DO YOU SUSPECT A GRAMINOID
(grass/sedge/rush) as the flowers
have no petals?
no > See Pocket Guide
probably a forb

yes (or at least try this route)

IS STEM HOLLOW (can be flattened)
& JOINTED (with solid nodes)

< yes

no

**DEFINITELY
A GRASS**
Poaceae

IS STEM SOLID, UNJOINTED
ROUND?
no >
IS STEM SOLID, UNJOINTED
TRIANGULAR?

yes   yes

probably RUSH but read on   probably SEDGE but read on

LVS MOSTLY
BASAL?
no – possibly SEDGE
no – possibly RUSH
LVS IN 3 RANKS
UP STEM?

yes   yes

RUSH even more likely!   SEDGE even more likely!

INDIV FLS MORE LIKE MONOCOT FORB?
(6 tepals, flower/capsule in centre)
INDIV FLS MORE LIKE GRASS
(single scale round flower/fruit)

go back to SEDGE   < no   yes   go back to RUSH   < no   yes

**DEFINITELY
A RUSH**
Juncaceae
**DEFINITELY
A SEDGE**
Cyperaceae

IS IT A GRASS, A SEDGE OR A RUSH?

GRASS STRUCTURE

Now we come to the grasses themselves, the family **Poaceae**. Rather than covering every detail, we will limit this study to the field characters you need to know in order to identify with reasonable confidence the 20 common species dealt with here.

The diagram opposite shows the structure of a grass plant. The inflorescence (flowerhead) is composed of spikelets (see various arrangements in the next section). Note where to find the ligule: pull the leaf-blade gently away from the stem – see right – and you will find the ligule at the junction (that is, at the junction of the blade and the sheath). At the bottom of page 8 are some examples of ligules: whether they are long or short, pointed or blunt etc can be a vital aid to ID. Always examine the ligule carefully, and look at several on the same plant as the top one may differ slightly from those lower down.

The diagram also shows the difference between stolons – overground – and rhizomes – underground – which can throw up new stems at a distance. Not all grasses have either of these and they may not be easy to see in any case. You should find you are able to do the ID in this book without them, but they can sometimes be an extra help to diagnosis.

On the right of the main diagram are some examples of spikelets. Each spikelet is enclosed by a pair of glumes, which are rather like the bracts seen in other flowering plants. The glumes on the wild oats in the photograph below are so large they hide the whole floret, but this isn't always the case. We don't really use glumes for ID in this book, but it is important to distinguish them from the florets inside. Some grasses will be awned: that is, various flower parts will have structures like delicate bristles. These can be long or short, bent or straight and so on, so take careful note.

GRASS STRUCTURE

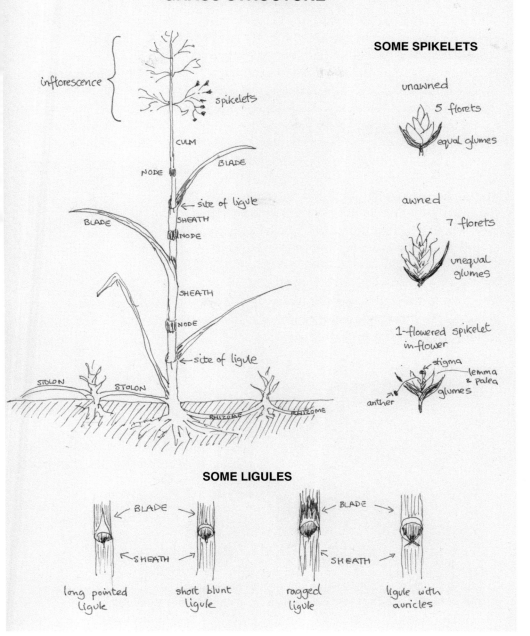

inflorescence

spikelets

CULM

NODE

BLADE

← site of ligule

SHEATH

NODE

BLADE

SHEATH

NODE

← site of ligule

STOLON

STOLON

RHIZOME

RHIZOME

SOME SPIKELETS

unawned

5 florets

equal glumes

awned

7 florets

unequal glumes

1-flowered spikelet in flower

stigma

lemma & palea

glumes

anther

SOME LIGULES

BLADE

SHEATH

long pointed ligule

short blunt ligule

BLADE

SHEATH

ragged ligule

ligule with auricles

GRASS INFLORESCENCE

The final diagram, opposite, shows the two main styles of inflorescence: spike-type (be careful not to confuse this term with 'spikelet'!) and panicle-type. Within the spike-type style there are four basic sub-types. There are just two sub-types of panicle. This is an essential piece of data for ID, so make sure you can tell your spikes from your panicles, your whorled from your branched panicles and so on, before you actually attempt to identify any grasses. I suggest you practice with any grass you find, simply deciding what type of inflorescence it has: don't go any further with attempts at ID until you have got this aspect sorted. After that, you can look at ligules, spikelets, awns and so on.

Spikelets can have one, two or many florets enclosed by the glumes: learning to recognise these differences, shown at the bottom of page 11, can be a big help for the ID of certain genera. However, if you are new to grasses, you are bound to find this quite tricky at first. Don't worry if you can't say exactly how many florets there are in a particular spikelet. With practice, you will find that one-flowered spikelets do look quite different from the others, so as long as you can tell 'one' from 'many' you will manage to ID most species.

A many-flowered grass

A one-flowered grass

Detail of one-flowered grass

GRASS INFLORESCENCE

SPIKE-TYPE – pedicels very short to nil

FLAT
SPIKES

HALF MOON   CYLINDRICAL

spikelets
broadside-on

spikelets
edgeways-on

PANICLE-TYPE –
pedicels long, branching

irregularly-
branched
panicle

whorled
panicle

FLOWERS PER SPIKELET

1-flowered
spikelets

2-flowered
spikelets

many-flowered
spikelets

Before you go on to try the flowchart itself, it might be a good idea to check whether you have grasped all the points you will be using to identify your specimen.

Are you sure it's a grass? Only one of the three images below shows a grass, so which one is it?

Of the two on the right, which is the **spike-like** inflorescence which is the **panicle-like**?

Can you say which of these two has spikelets **broadside-on** and which has spikelets **edgeways-on?**

Which of the grasses below has a **whorled panicle** and which has an **irregularly branched panicle?**

For each of these, would you saying you are looking at a grass with **one-flowered spikelets** or a grass with **many-flowered spikelets?**

OUR TWENTY COMMON SPECIES

Typical neutral grassland

Agrostis capillaris	Common Bent
Agrostis stolonifera	Creeping Bent
Agrostis vinealis	Brown Bent
Alopecuris pratensis	Meadow Foxtail
Anthoxanthum odoratum	Sweet Vernal-grass
Arrhenatherum elatius	False Oat-grass
Bromus hordaceus	Soft Brome
Cynosurus cristatus	Crested Dog's-tail
Dactylis glomerata	Cocksfoot
Festuca rubra	Red Fescue
Elymus repens	Common Couch
Deschampsia cespitosa	Tufted Hair-grass
Holcus lanatus	Yorkshire Fog
Hordeum murinum	Wall Barley
Lolium perenne	Perennial Rye-grass
Phleum pratense	Timothy
Poa annua	Annual Meadow-grass
Poa pratensis	Smooth Meadow-grass
Poa trivialis	Rough Meadow-grass
Schedonorus arundinaceus	Tall Fescue

AND SOME 'EXTRAS' – species closely related to those in the main flowchart, but found in slightly different habitats.

Agrostis canina	Velvet Bent
Alopecurus geniculatus	Marsh Foxtail
Avenella flexuosa	Wavy Hair-grass
Elymus caninus	Bearded Couch
Festuca ovina	Sheep's Fescue
Holcus mollis	Creeping soft-grass
Schedonorus pratensis	Meadow Fescue
Other Bromes & Fescues	

Different grasses will be found in these woodland, mountain and wetland habitats.

TIMES AND SEASONS

Look for grasses in flower from late Spring onwards, though of course the actual date depends on how far north or south you are. The flowchart points out some species which are early-flowering and likely to have gone over – looking browner and feeling drier – when the majority are still in flower.   Many grasses are easier to identify in the early morning when the inflorescence is more likely to be open: panicles can look quite different when closed up (see below). If you are not sure of spike vs panicle, spread the inflorescence out to see whether the pedicels (spikelet stems) are long, which indicates a panicle. or very short to non-existent, indicating a spike.

You might think there were several different grasses in this picture, but it's all Yorkshire Fog, at various stages of opening. Yorkshire Fog also varies in colour – sometimes white, sometimes pink, sometimes mauve.

FLOWCHART TO TWENTY GRASSES

Once you have studied the diagrams in the introduction for a while, and become used to the terminology of grasses and the sorts of characters you need to examine in order to achieve a positive identification, it is time to move on to the main flowchart.

This is not a key to grasses in the usual sense: it only covers these 20 species (plus brief notes on a few look-alikes from other habitats). So it only needs deal with the features that distinguish these 20 from each other. Exhaustive keys, such as are found in books like Hubbard and Cope & Gray (see booklist at the end), are dauntingly complicated because they have to cover all British native grasses, numbering about 160 species.

What fun you have in store for you when you have mastered these 20 and a few others besides, and can go on to try your hand at identifying the other 140 or so as you encounter them!

In the flowchart that follows, consider the questions in order – your answer will direct you either to the most likely species, or to a further question.
NB You will probably need your x10 lens to see some of the details.

Q1 INFLORESCENCE

Is the inflorescence a SPIKE or spike-like?   If yes, GO TO Q2
(very short pedicels or none at all)

Or is the inflorescence a PANICLE ?   If yes, GO TO Q5
(long pedicels/branches)

Q2 SPIKE

Is the spike FLAT ?   If yes, GO TO Q3
Or is the spike CYLINDRICAL ?   If yes, GO TO Q4
Or is the spike HALF-MOON shaped in cross-section?

'front' view

'back' view

The only common species like this is
==Crested Dogstail==
==*Cynosurus cristatus*==

<u>Check</u>: spikelets in pairs
– one fertile, one sterile.

Q3   FLAT SPIKE

Are the spikelets BROADSIDE ON to the stem?   Or are they EDGEWAYS ON?

Most likely species is

==Common Couch==
==*Elymus repens*==

<u>Check</u>: may have short awns, leaves hairy, ligule virtually non-existent.

Most likely species is

==Perennial Ryegrass==
==*Lolium erenne*==

<u>Check</u>: never awned, leaves hairless, very short ligule.

Very like Common Couch, but long-awned, is Bearded Couch *Elymus caninus*

Q4 CYLINDRICAL SPIKE

Are there NUMEROUS LONG STRAIGHT AWNS? Most probable candidate is

Check: Mainly found by paths, on
disturbed ground etc.

Wall Barley
Hordeum murinum

Or does each individual floret have TWO LONG BENT AWNS?

Most likely species is
Sweet Vernal Grass
Anthoxanthum odoratum

Check: very early flowering –
soon turning brown, shaggy appearance.

Or do the florets have 'HORNS' (you may need your lens here)?

There is only one common grass like this:
Timothy
Phleum pratense

Check: anthers usually (not always) purple.
Timothy flowers quite a bit later in the year than
Meadow Foxtail (below).

Or do they have a SINGLE INCONSPICUOUS AWN?

Most likely to be

Meadow Foxtail
Alopecurus pratensis

Check: it is essential to examine the florets – fold the spike in half to
see the florets clearly – as the spikes (see right) are so similar to those
of Timothy, except the anthers are usually (not always) orange.

Marsh Foxtail *Alopecurus geniculatus,* found in damp and marshy
places, is similar but the stem has a bent 'knee' and a much longer ligule.

Q5 PANICLE

Is the panicle IRREGULARLY BRANCHED?   If yes, GO TO Q6

Or is the panicle WHORLED?   If yes, GO TO Q9

Q6   IRREGULARLY BRANCHED PANICLE

Are the spikelets
FLATTENED?

If yes, GO TO Q7

Or are the spikelets in LARGE BUSHY CLUMPS?

There is not much else like this; it will be

Cocksfoot
Dactylis glomerata

Check: tall, coarse, densely-tufted plant with broad leaves.

Q7 FLATTENED SPIKELETS

Is the whole plant DENSELY HAIRY, the spikelets OVAL?

A good candidate is
Soft Brome
Bromus hordaceus

Check: long awns, ligule finely toothed,
hairs giving a silvery appearance.

Other Bromes have similar shaped spikelets, almost all with long awns.

Or is the plant mostly HAIRLESS,
the spikelets more V-SHAPED?

If yes, GO TO Q8

Q8 MOSTLY HAIRLESS, V-SHAPED SPIKELETS

Are the basal leaves BRISTLE-LIKE?

One of the commonest of all grasses – though very variable and with many subspecies – is

Red Fescue
Festuca rubra

Check: fairly short awns, ligule very short and blunt, stem leaves narrow but flat.

If stem leaves bristle-like too, probably Sheep's Fescue *Festuca ovina,* more likely in the uplands. All Fescues have similar shaped spikelets.

Or are the basal leaves BROAD AND FLAT?

If this a very tall plant, chances are it is

Tall Fescue
Schedonorus arundinaceus

Check: short ligule with hairy auricles

Similar, but less common, is Meadow Fescue *Schedonorus pratensis* which has no awns and hairless auricles.

Q9 WHORLED PANICLE

Are the spikelets 1-FLOWERED?   If yes, GO TO Q10

Or are the spikelets 2-FLOWERED?   If yes, GO TO Q11

Or are the spikelets MANY-FLOWERED?   If yes, GO TO Q14

In this habitat, these are almost certain to be Bents – *Agrostis* species. For easiest diagnosis, examine the ligule. That said, *Agrostis* is a notoriously difficult genus: you may prefer to say '*Agrostis agg*' and leave teasing out the species until later.

Is the ligule SHORT & BLUNT?
Best candidate is

Common Bent
Agrostis capillaris

Check: branches bare at bases, no awns

Or is the ligule LONG & POINTED?
If there are also SHORT AWNS, this is likely to be

Brown Bent
Agrostis vinealis
Check: branches bare at bases

Velvet Bent *A. canina* is almost identical but has stolons and is found in more marshy or woody places.

Or is the ligule LONG BUT BLUNTER?
Especially if NO AWNS, this is probably

Creeping Bent
Agrostis stolonifera

Check: branches more crowded to base, stolons in evidence (search at ground level).

Note: 2-flowered spikelets are notoriously hard to see. If Qs 12 & 13 don't seem to yield the right answer, go on to look at Q14.

Are the panicles DENSER, with SHORTER BRANCHES?   If yes, GO TO Q12
Or are the panicles LOOSER, with LONGER BRANCHES?   If yes, GO TO Q13

Q12 DENSER PANICLES, SHORTER BRANCHES

Is the plant SOFTLY HAIRY all over, with a PINKISH or WHITISH appearance?

This is very likely to be

Yorkshire Fog

Holcus lanatus

Check: awns very tiny. N.B. You will soon get the distinctive 'jizz' of Yorkshire Fog and no longer need to count florets.

Creeping Soft-grass *Holcus mollis* (woodland) is similar but has 'hairy knees' (above right).

Or is the plant tall, BROWNISH GREEN (probably), with LONG BENT AWNS?

A good candidate is

False Oat Grass

Arrhenatherum elatius

Check: probably only hairy at top of sheath (see right), glumes transparent and unequal.

Q13 LOOSER PANICLES, LONGER BRANCHES

This is probably a Hair Grass *Deschamspia* – tall, silvery grasses with long drooping branches. In NEUTRAL grassland, this is most likely to be

Tufted Hair Grass
Deschampsia cespitosa

Check: flat, rough leaves in dense tussock, ligule very long and pointed.

In a more ACID heathy or woody habitat it is more probably Wavy Hair Grass *Avenella flexuosa*
(right) which has leaves more bristle-like, ligule shorter.

Q14 MANY-FLOWERED SPIKELETS

These are likely to be in the very common genus of Meadow Grasses *Poa*.
(NB. Some specimens of Poa may be 2-flowered)

Rub the sheaths gently **upwards**, and also examine the ligules:
Do the sheaths feel ROUGH, are the ligules LONG AND POINTED? This is

Rough Meadow Grass
Poa trivialis

Check: favours damper ground,
spikelets slightly smaller than
P. pratensis

Or are the sheaths SMOOTH, the ligules SHORT, otherwise
very like Rough Meadow Grass? Then it is likely to be (wait for it)

Smooth Meadow Grass
Poa pratensis

Check: favours drier ground, spikelets
tend to be slightly longer

Or are the sheaths SMOOTH, the ligules BLUNT, and the whole plant in a
SMALL TUFT on a path, waste ground etc? This will probably be

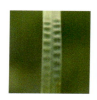

Annual Meadow Grass
Poa annua

Check: leaves often transversely wrinkled. In flower
all year round. Only two branches at lowest node.

Note: If you seem to have come to a dead end, trying going back to Q11 in case your
grass is 2-flowered. Or you may have a less common species – carry on reading . . .

WHAT NEXT?

Some of the species here are more difficult to tease out than others, but because they are all so common, you will soon find that you recognise quite a few of them by 'jizz'. In that case, you can just run a quick check to make sure your identification is correct. Others can be a bit of a challenge even to experienced botanists, so don't feel downhearted if you simply can't work out a particular specimen – we've all been there!

Because grasses are admitted by all to be considerably harder to pin down than forbs, one has to be that much more careful about jumping to conclusions. if in doubt, you could always check with an expert if you have one to hand. Especially if you are recording – it is better to record nothing at all than to record in error.

If you find yourself seriously into grass ID, it may be time to begin using guides that are exhaustive, as opposed to dealing with just the commonest species, or with species of a particular habitat or found in a particular region. In the booklist that follows, 'Hubbard' is pretty much the bible of the grass domain: the standard text for more than half a century. In other words, what Hubbard says will be accepted by virtually everyone else.

Cope & Gray (first published in 2009) is in some ways an update on Hubbard, taking into account recent taxonomic and nomenclature changes. It also has a different approach to keys: instead of starting from scratch, as it were, it takes a hierarchical line: grasses are first divided into tribes, then into genera, and only then into species. Some people find this very helpful, though admittedly there are others whom it doesn't suit. The authors also specifically state that their book is written chiefly for ID purposes, so some features that don't help with ID are omitted, which can make for greater clarity.

Francis Rose's Colour Identification Guide covers sedges and rushes as well as grasses. Unlike the first two books, it doesn't show every detail of every species. However, the keys are (in my opinion, at any rate) much easier to follow. The keys are accompanied by many helpful little diagrams to explain the distinctions in question, as are the definitions in the glossary. The main illustrations in colour (left) are lively and natural in a way that the technical drawings of Hubbard and Cope & Gray are not intended to be.

But there is nothing like hands-on practice for getting to grips with grasses. So do keep a lookout for workshops, field meetings, experts to consult and all other means – including constant fieldwork of your own – for learning more about these ever-fascinating plants.

FURTHER READING

COPE & GRAY **Grasses of the British isles** *BSBI Handbook*

The latest and most complete guide to British grass ID, with relatively straightforward keys.

HUBBARD **Grasses** *3rd Edition, Pelican*

The classic authoritative work on British grasses, though keys notoriously hard to follow!

FRANCIS ROSE **Colour Identification Guide to the Grasses, Sedges, Rushes and Ferns** of the British Isles and NW Europe *Viking*

Easy-to-follow keys, great illustrations, descriptions briefer than the above. Expensive!

FITTER **Grasses, Sedges, Rushes & Ferns** *Collins Guide*

Good drawings, brief descriptions, maps; multi-access key is not universally popular.

HARRINGTON **How to Identify Grasses & Grasslike Plants** *Swallow Press*

This is an American book, but that isn't relevant here because it is about the universal characteristics of grasses. The only book of its kind and very helpful for beginners.

PHILLIPS **Grasses, Ferns, Mosses & Lichens** *Pan*

Photographic guide useful as such, descriptions minimal.

PRICE **A Field Guide to Grasses, Sedges & Rushes** *Species Recovery Trust*

ID by habitat, excellent detailed photos of common species, descriptions very brief.

FSC **Grass Identification Guide** *Field Studies Council*

Fold-out chart to 30 common grasses, labelled illustrations only.

Annual Beard-grass
Polypogon monspeliensis

Southern Beard-grass
Polypogon maritimus

Grasses etc also covered in:

STREETER ET AL Collins Wildflower Guide – easy-to-follow keys, drawings (right) small, descriptions fairly brief, but the advantage is in having only one book to carry!

POLAND & CLEMENT Vegetative Key to the British Flora *BSBI* – good choice when no inflorescence present, awe-inspiring glossary.

Some online resources

www.bsbi.org/identification – scroll down to bottom right 'TEP files' for detailed accounts of individual grass genera, with excellent photos by Peter Gateley, some of which have been used here.

www.countrysideinfo.co.uk/grass_id – accurate and detailed explanation of grass structure and the process of identification.

www.naturespot.org/home – scroll down Species Galleries to Grasses, Sedges & Rushes. Good photos, brief description, but local to central England.